CHALLENGER SKETCHBOOK

B. SHEPHARD'S SKETCHBOOK
of the
H.M.S. CHALLENGER EXPEDITION
1872-1874

Prepared and edited for publication by
Harris B. Stewart, Jr. and J. Welles Henderson

Published by
PHILADELPHIA MARITIME MUSEUM
1972
Distributed by the NEW YORK GRAPHIC SOCIETY, Ltd. Greenwich, Connecticut

Preface

The *Challenger* sketchbook was discovered in 1968 in an antique shop in Boston, Massachusetts, by J. Welles Henderson. In his capacity as president of the Philadelphia Maritime Museum, Mr. Henderson showed the sketchbook to Harris B. Stewart, Jr., a member of the museum's Underwater Advisory Board. Both felt the drawings add a delightful artistic postscript to the volumes already written about what is still considered the greatest of all oceanographic expeditions. The 100th anniversary of the *Challenger* voyage seemed a fitting time to share the sketchbook with oceanographers everywhere. Consequently, Mr. Stewart volunteered to undertake the formidible task of research and preparation of the descriptive content.

In reading through two of the logs maintained during the expedition to try to obtain some background for each of the paintings, it was soon realized that the journals kept by men aboard the H.M.S. *Challenger* during the trip provided much more of the true flavor of the expedition than could otherwise be recaptured, almost one hundred years later. They were even better than the official narrative of the expedition contained in the First Part of Volume 1 of Sir C. Wyville Thomson and John Murray's *"Report on the Scientific Results of the Voyage of H.M.S. CHALLENGER during the years 1873-7"* (H.M. Stationery Office, London, 1885). With this rationale, this volume has shamelessly borrowed from the extremely informative and well written journals of the Assistant Engineer, W.J.J. Spry, R.N. (*The Cruise of Her Majesty's Ship "Challenger"*, Harper and Brothers, New York, 1877), and of Sub-Lieutenant Lord George C. Campbell, R.N. (*Log-Letters of the "Challenger"*, MacMillan & Co., New York, 1877).

Any student of oceanography or of the history of science in general, would do well to read these two accounts of a great expedition. They supplement each other nicely, one going into great detail of incidents on the expedition which the other brushes over only casually or omits altogether. The descriptions of Spry and Lord Campbell provide a contemporary descriptive background to most of the watercolors, for as members of the officer-crew complement of the *Challenger*, they, like the artist, were more interested in the ports than in the scientific work aboard. In all fairness, however, it must be added that in both journals the authors exhibit a commendable familiarity with and respect for the scientific activities aboard.

For some unknown reason, the voluminous official documentation on the *Challenger* Expedition nowhere lists the crew members by name and rate. Scientists and ship's officers are well known and regularly referred to, but the members of the crew appear consigned to anonymity. For this reason, it was extremely difficult to discover if one B. Shephard was even aboard the *Challenger*.

No pertinent records could be found in the United States. Through the excellent assistance of Dr. J.D.H. Wiseman of the British Museum, the first glimmer of hope was seen when he discovered in the Murray Library—the collection of John Murray's papers relating to the expedition—a penciled note to one "Shepherd" (spelled with an "e") in connection with some lithographic plates. Shortly thereafter, Commander D.P.D. Scott, M.B.E. (R.N.) of the British Hydrographic Department who had also been working on the problem, wrote to report the complete success of his research with the files of Naval Service Certificates in the Public Record Office in London. Commander Scott has graciously had copies made of some seven sheets of official records all relating to the service of Benjamin Shephard (also spelled with an "e" in one place) who did indeed serve on the *Challenger*.

It is with great personal pleasure and a humble respect for the oceanographers who were iron men sailing in wooden ships that we bring to the oceanographers of the Twentieth Century, a new insight into the greatest oceanographic expedition that man has yet undertaken.

J. Welles Henderson
Harris B. Stewart, Jr.

Summer 1972

Introduction

Benjamin Shephard was a cooper aboard the entire voyage of H.M.S. *Challenger* from November 1872 until May 1876.

Like the sailors on most oceanographic expeditions, those aboard the H.M.S. *Challenger*, although intrigued by the work of the scientists, were more interested in the ports which punctuated the long periods of observations at sea. Thus Shephard, with few exceptions, concentrated on painting not the scientific work at sea but rather the *Challenger* at her various ports of call. Starting with one showing the ship's departure from Gibraltar on January 26, 1873, Shephard's watercolors cover Madeira, St. Thomas, Bermuda, Halifax, St. Michael's, St. Vincent, St. Paul's Rocks, Fernando Noronha, Tristan de Cunha, Capetown, Prince Edward Island, Crozet Island, Kerguelen Island, and McDonald Island. In addition, there is a delightful and fanciful dredging scene, but this plus one of a storm and six reflecting his fascination with icebergs, are the only ones of his 34 not related to specific landfalls.

Shephard's renditions of the ship itself, are extremely accurate with the single exception that—as a true man of sail—he frequently refuses to show in his paintings that the *Challenger* had a stack. Although she was a spar-decked corvette of 2306 tons displacement, she did have a 1234-horsepower engine that was used from time to time during the expedition. Generally when on-station, she would drop her canvas and stay head-on into the seas maintaining station with power.

Other than in the paintings themselves, Shephard has a delightful disregard for accuracy. The English vessel towed by the *Challenger* into St. Thomas on March 23rd, 1873, for example, was named the *Varuna*. Shephard, however, (in Sketch No. 5) not only called her the "*Baruner*", but missed the date by four days and even spelled the name of the island incorrectly (St. Thomass). To his casual approach to the accuracy of dates and spelling must also be added a rare dedication to the doctrine of inconsistency. Sketches 25, 26 and 27 all are of the ship's activities at Kerguelen Island, yet in no two of them does he spell the island's name the same way. It is Kerguelen (No. 25), Kerguelan (No. 26), and Kergulen (No. 27).

These, however, are the comments of an incurable nitpicker. Shephard's watercolors are magnificently done and extremely well preserved. They provide to oceanographers a new feel for and insight into the *Challenger* Expedition. This expedition, some one hundred years later, is still regarded as the greatest marine science expedition of all time. Through Shephard's paintings, today's oceanographers will realize that the *Challenger* Expedition was not too different from ours of today. We feel closer to Sir Charles Wyville Thomson, Moseley, Murray, and the others of the scientific party and to Captain George S. Nares, his officers and crew because of Shephard's translation of his love for the sea, a ship, and an expedition into a series of watercolors that have been lost and now are found.

Benjamin Shephard was born September 18th, 1841, at Brixton in Surrey. He entered service on May 9th, 1862, at the age of 20, and when he signed up for a ten-year period of service the following October, the records show that he stood 5 feet 7 inches, was of fair complexion, with brown hair and blue eyes. He entered as a cooper and two years later, was promoted to coopers crew. Evidently he found work not particularly to his liking, as he was demoted and promoted several times during his 25-year career. His final rate, however, was still cooper. On October 28th, 1867, he deserted but returned the following October 3rd, to sign up again for ten years. His first assignment was a 15-week sentence for desertion, but from then on, for the rest of his career, he served on many ships as cooper or coopers crew.

Shephard was assigned to H.M.S. *Challenger* November 15th, 1872 at the age of 31, as a cooper. Again he was promoted to coopers crew on December 1, 1874, but was demoted back to cooper again on June 1st, 1875, while the *Challenger* was in Japan. The expedition returned to England the last week of May, 1876, and Shephard was transferred to H.M.S. *Pembroke* on June 12th, 1876. In succession, he served on the H.M.S. *Pembroke* (June to August 1876), H.M.S. *Penelope* (August 1876–March 1879), H.M.S. *Pembroke* again (March–October 1879), H.M.S. *Cornus* (October 1879 to March 1884), back to the H.M.S. *Pembroke* (March 1884 to January 1885), H.M.S. *Tyne* (January 1885 to June 1887), and finally the H.M.S. *Nelson*. He transferred from the H.M.S. *Tyne* to the H.M.S. *Nelson* on June 20th, 1887 at Albany, W. Australia, where he died of "phthisis" (pulmonary tuberculosis) three days later at the age of 45.

The 34 watercolors of this sketchbook cover only one third of the total *Challenger* expedition, between January 1873 and February of 1874. It is hoped that Shephard was able to continue his watercolors during the remaining two years of the expedition, and that additional sketchbooks are waiting to be found and appreciated for what they are.

1 *"What We Get and How We Got It"*

Of all of Shephard's watercolors, only this one has the delightful and fanciful touch to lift it above the others. The idea of mermaids "helping" with the dredging also appears in one of the small sketches by the Expedition Artist, J. J. Wild, and is used as a page filler in the official Expedition Report. Other parallels between the paintings of Shephard and the works of Wild suggest that the two men occasionally worked together or at least were familiar with each other's work.

As on the *Challenger's* present day counterparts, dredging is not always successful. Of her first attempt to dredge, Spry reports (pp. 12-13): "After this the dredge was put over and lowered to the bottom, where it was allowed to remain some hours, the vessel slowly drifting onward. On hauling in it was found turned upside-down, and in a lovely tangle. Dredging was resumed on the 2nd January, but with no better results, for the dredge fouled the bottom, and eventually the rope parted and some 3000 fathoms were lost."

They soon switched to a trawl in their attempts to collect bottom life and obtained better results. As Campbell puts it (pp. 4-5): "We dredged several times with entire success in depths under 1,000 fathoms. The mud! ye gods, imagine a cart full of whitish mud, filled with the minutest shells, poured all wet and sticky and slimey on to some clean planks, and then you may have some faint idea of how globigerina mud appears to us. In this the naturalists paddle and wade about, putting spadefulls into successively finer and finer sieves, till nothing remains but the minute shells, &c.

"But this cruise is memorable in the annals of the CHALLENGER, as during it we first tried the trawl instead of the dredge, which revolutionized eventually our dredging system. We had a trawl or two on board—the ordinary beam trawl—which somebody proposed trying; so it was forthwith rigged up and sent down in 620 fms., after the dredge had come up with the usual hundredweight or two of mud and a few animals. And lo! in the trawl there appeared three fish of two different and exceedingly rare species, ghastly objects, bursting and blown out like balloons, with eyes starting out from their heads. There were also beautiful corals, two feet high, and brilliantly phosphorescent when stirred in a darkened room."

To those of the ship's company not involved in the actual dredging operation, their day ran something like this (Spry, pp. 56-57): "During the time of sounding and dredging, the ship's company not specially employed on these operations have been mustered at division, attended prayers, and engaged during the forenoon in their various and requisite duties. At noon, dinner is piped, and although consisting, as it usually does, of either salt junk and duff, or fat, greasy salt pork and pea soup, there are few men healthier than the sailor. Grog-time comes next (when half a gill of rum with two parts of water is supplied to each man), and, with the hour for smoking, constitutes a pleasant break in the day. Duty is resumed again at 1.30, and various drills occupy the afternoon until 4.30, when all hands assemble at their stations, with rifle, cutlass, and pistol for inspection by their divisional officer.

"The inspection over (we will presume the dredge to be up, and the excitement of the haul subsided), 'Hands! make sail,' is the pipe. Steam is dispensed with, in a short time the sail is all spread, and with a favouring breeze we are running on our course at an eight-knot speed. Supper is now prepared, consisting of tea and biscuit, after which, until 9, smoking is permitted, hammocks having been piped down at 7.30. The commanding officer usually goes the round of the decks, to ascertain that all is correct, when those off duty are expected to turn-in their hammocks, and so ends the day and its duties."

Gibraltar was the *Challenger's* second port of call after her departure from Portsmouth on 21 December, 1872, a stop having been made at Lisbon. Campbell brushes aside the eight days at Gibraltar with little comment (p. 5): "We stayed at Gibraltar till the 26th, during which period nothing occurred of which I need write to you; and besides, everybody knows all about 'old Gib,' which was doubly pleasant to us with its brilliant sunshine, and gardens a blaze of flowers, coming from England in winter, and south-westerly gales in the Channel and Lisbon."

Spry, on the other hand, assumes that no one knows anything of "old Gib," and describes the Rock and its settlements and bastions in great detail. Of their departure on 26 January, 1873, he says (pp. 25-26): "While at Gibraltar, a new survey was made of the inner mole, the ship's chronometers rated, and magnetic observations obtained. On 26th January we left the anchorage and proceeded round Europa Point, and as the day was well advanced, hastened on so as to get through the Straits before dark. After passing the Pillars of Hercules, the wind freshened considerably, and the intention of making a short detour from our course so as to visit Tangiers had to be abandoned. Early next morning we passed the most southerly point of Europe, and as we steamed on, we gradually lost sight of the coast, which was beautifully illuminated by the rising sun, affording us the last glimpse of the Old World."

Shephard's painting shows the stack on the *Challenger*. She is obviously headed out under power and will up sail once clear of the lee of the Rock.

3 *"H.M.S. CHALLENGER leaving Madeira, 1873"*

This sketch is not only one of the two showing no date, but is also one of those showing the *Challenger* under steam rather than sail. Shephard evidently enjoyed the ship's reflection in water and this appears in many of the sketches. Even though the sea surface shown elsewhere in the painting and the plume of smoke trailing aft of the *Challenger* suggest something other than the glassy surface required for such a reflection, this obviously did not bother Shephard, and the clear reflection of the hull and masts adds to the interest of the painting.

On leaving Gibraltar the *Challenger* had sailed west and picked up the sounding line they had terminated off Lisbon. As they worked their way southwest and south, the weather moderated and the scientists aboard had a series of highly successful trawls in depths of 1,100 to 2,125 fathoms.

The ship arrived at the island of Madeira February 3, 1873. Campbell mentions the visit only in passing (p. 6): "Madeira was, as it always is, delicious and lovely." Spry, on the other hand, devotes some five pages to a description of the land, its history, its vegetation, even the dress of the inhabitants. Of the bay, shown in Shephard's painting, Spry reports (p. 29): "On the morning of February 3rd, we arrived and anchored in Funchal Bay, just to the south of the Loo Rock, the only place of shelter at this season of the year, the open roadstead affording but little protection against the prevailing winds. The weather was fortunately very fine, and we were enabled to coal in safety. Com-

ing in from the monotonous sea, the first impressions of Funchal are delightful and striking with its luxurious gardens smiling with gorgeous flowers, and its mountain-sides cultivated almost to their summits with beautiful plants. Nature exhibits herself here with such varied charms that imagination can scarcely picture a lovelier scene."

The actual departure depicted by Shephard is mentioned only briefly by Spry (p. 32): "During the two days of our stay at Funchal the weather was very favourable for coaling, which was satisfactorically finished, and on the 5th February we proceeded out of the bay, and with a favouring breeze, were soon off the 'Desertas,' a group of barren rocks about 11 miles S.E. of Madeira."

It is interesting that there are no sketches covering the period from the departure at Madeira on February 5 until the ship's arrival at St. Thomas in the Virgin Islands on March 16th. It was not that there were no coasts to sketch for the *Challenger* stopped at Santa Cruz (Teneriffe) and made a close-in pass at Sombrero Island in the Virgin Islands, their first landfall in the West Indies. The *Challenger* was extremely busy on her crossing of the Atlantic, and it is quite possible that Shephard was just too active and too tired when hammocks were piped down at 7:30 to indulge in his extra curricular painting.

"H.M.S. CHALLENGER Entering St. Thomass, March 16th, 1873"

The last port of call before St. Thomas in the Virgin Islands had been Teneriffe over a month before. The crossing of the Atlantic had been relatively calm and highly productive. As Lord Campbell summarizes the crossing (p. 15): "We left Teneriffe on Feb. the 14th, and sailed westward across the Atlantic in the trade-wind regions with fresh breezes and beautiful weather, to St. Thomas's in the West Indies, distant about 2,700 miles, arriving there March the 16th. We sounded at about every 120 miles, and dredged at every 300, taking 22 deep-sea soundings, and 13 dredgings in depths varying from 1,420 to 3,150 fms.— the deepest water on this section."

He goes on to describe the island of St. Thomas with something less than enchantment (p. 17): "On the 24th we left the least pretty, the least typical, the most disappointing West Indian island I know of the many I have seen. St. Thomas is associated in Europeans' ears with tremendous hurricanes and epidemics of yellow fever. The first of these the Danish Officials and inhabitants have it not in their power to alter; but the second they have mitigated, if not entirely suppressed by cutting channels through certain coral reefs in their harbour, thereby causing a tidal circulation where was absolutely none before. St. Thomas is not a cheering place for an enthusiastic abolitionist to study the negro in a state of freedom. What were once sugar and cotton plantations is now covered with scrub, for the negroes will not work there while constant mail steamers come in for coals, at which, in a very few hours, they can earn enough to keep them for many days. Women work at the coaling too like horses, and the sight altogether is not an edifying one."

Spry, however, evidently had a more enjoyable time ashore, for he is less gloomy in his description (pp. 58-60): "On the morning of the 16th the island of St. Thomas (one of the Virgin group) was in sight; and later in the day we anchored in the outer harbour. The island of St. Thomas being usually very unhealthy, it was decided to anchor in the outer harbour, or Gregorie Channel. Here we swung ship, rated chronometers, and filled up with coal.

"Naturally enough, after being a month at sea, most were anxious for a run on shore. We found the country and scenery pretty; the lofty hills were varied in colour, and appeared to be thickly wooded with a variety of trees, all green and tempting, as far as the eye could reach.

"The town, named Charlotte Amalia, has no pretensions to size or elegance. It is, however, most picturesquely situated along the northern shore of the island, backed up by high hills, and having a curious saddle-shaped mountain running through its centre, terminating in two peaks, some 1525 feet in height. . . . A pleasant week had passed, several excursions had been made to the adjacent islands of Sombrero and St. John's, where not only dredging and sounding but good shooting were obtained."

5 *"H.M.S. CHALLENGER Towing the Abandoned Ship BARUNER Into St. Thomass on March 19th, 1873"*

Many oceanographic expeditions have been sidetracked for short periods to go to the assistance of a ship in distress, and the *Challenger* Expedition was no exception. As written up in the official narrative of the Expedition (Thomson and Murray, Vol. 1, p. 130): "It having been reported during the stay that a distressed British ship had anchored in the sound between the islands of St. Thomas and St. John, the ship proceeded to her assistance and towed her into harbour. She proved to be the VARUNA, an iron ship of 1300 tons, abandoned by the crew two months previously, about 350 miles N.N.E. of Bermuda; she was taken charge of by the mate and nine of the crew of the ship ROUNDTREE, and navigated to St. Thomas, having only her foremast and foretopmast standing. The men deserve great credit for bringing the VARUNA to port, and it is to be hoped that they got a handsome amount of salvage, although they distrusted the motives of the CHALLENGER in coming to their assistance, thinking they were to be deprived of some of their hardly-earned recompense, and had to be reassured on that point before the vessel was taken in tow."

Shephard shows the *Varuna*—or *"Baruner"*, as he incorrectly calls her—with the foremast and the foretopmast standing as described by Thompson and Murray, but he also shows her mainmast and mizzenmast as standing. That only the lower two sections of the fore remained is also borne out by Spry, who described the *Varuna* by writing (p. 61): "We learnt that she left New York in January last, and through falling in with very stormy weather had lost her main and mizen masts, and nearly all her sails, before she was abandoned to her fate." Perhaps the other two masts were added by Shephard for his own reasons, or perhaps they were jury-rigged by the men of the *Roundtree* to help her to St. Thomas. The former, somehow, seems to be the more logical explanation; for he might as well rig her as he wishes, since he missed the date of the incident by four days (it happened the 23rd not the 19th of March), he missed the real name of the ship, and misspelled the name of the island to which she was towed.

H.M.S. CHALLENGER. TOWING. THE. ABANDONED. SHIP. BARUNER. INTO. S.T. THOMASS. ON. MARCH. 18TH. 1873.

6 "H.M.S. CHALLENGER Entering Bermuda, April 3rd, 1873"

Lord Campbell found Bermuda to be as lacking in enchantment as St. Thomas seemed to be and reports his impressions thusly (p. 18): "In the shallow water close around Bermuda we got some good hauls, new species of sea-urchins, starfish, sponges; and on April the 4th we steamed into Bermuda through the narrow, tortuous channel in the outlying coral-reefs. Bermuda is remarkable for its varied vegetation, its admirable tomatoes and onions, its epidemics of yellow fever, its damp cold weather at some seasons, its intense heat at another, its geology, its numerous caves, its villanous mosquitoes, its fish, its unique but monotonous loveliness, its great importance as a naval and military station, and, I would add, its intense wearisomeness."

Shephard's painting of the *Challenger's* approach to Bermuda seems to follow more the description of the island by Spry than that of Lord Campbell. Spry seemed quite intrigued with the approach to the island, and wrote (pp. 62-64): "For several days soundings showed an average depth of 2800 fathoms, with a red-clay bottom; this continued until within about 100 miles of Bermuda, when we again came upon the grey ooze. On the 3rd of April land was in sight; and as we approached the Bermudas, which are mere specks on the chart of the wide Atlantic, one is immediately struck with their somewhat dull and sombre aspect; the land nowhere rising to a greater height than 260 feet (where the lighthouse is situated), and by far the greater part not being more than from 25 to 50 feet above the sea-level. We hove-to for the night, and for a portion of the next day were engaged sounding and dredging around the reefs in a depth of 400 fathoms on a coral clay bottom; the results were, as is usually the case in the proximity of coral reefs, extremely poor, the coral sand *debris* being apparently unfavourable to the development of animal life.

"On its conclusion, we closed on the land; and as we stopped off St. George's for the pilot to navigate the vessel through the intricate and dangerous narrows between the reefs, it was indeed a pretty sight. Seemingly nothing could have been more romantic than the little harbour stretched out before us; the variety and beauty of the islets scattered about; the clearness of the water; the number of boats and small vessels cruising between the islands, sailing from one cedar-grove to another, made up as charming a picture as could well be imagined."

It was this "charming picture" that Shephard chose to paint.

H.M.S.CHALLENGER ENTERING BERMUDA. APRIL 3RD 1873.

7

"H.M.S. CHALLENGER Leaving Halifax, Nova Scotia, May 19th, 1873, and H.M.S. ROYAL ALFRED Cheering Us Out"

After making an oceanographic section across the Gulf Stream between Bermuda and New York, the *Challenger* changed course for Halifax some 100 miles off Long Island. She sounded and dredged her way up the coast, crossing "curious veins of warm and cold water" (Campbell, p. 22), to arrive at Halifax, Nova Scotia, in the afternoon of May 9, 1873.

Evidently the crew was glad to be ashore where the countryside was more like their homeland and where the inhabitants greeted them most warmly. Spry described Halifax and Dartmouth in considerable detail and with great affection.

Even as today's oceanographic ships are often opened for inspection at foreign ports and local scientists invited aboard, so too was the *Challenger* at Halifax. Spry concludes his description of the ship's stay at Halifax thusly (pp. 74-75):

"During our stay, as we lay alongside the Naval Yard, every facility was afforded our Halifax friends to visit the ship. Many availed themselves of the opportunity, and evidenced the greatest desire to see and examine the many submarine wonders that had up to this date been collected.

"The members of the Halifax Institute of Natural Science mustered in strong numbers, and appeared to take a special interest in the work already accomplished.

"The blind crustacean zoophytes, the varieties of rare and new forms of corals and sponges, were well scanned; while for the geologists, amongst other things attracting their attention, was a large boulder, which had been brought up in the dredge some 300 miles south of the coast. This was carefully examined, and eventually recognized as a piece of Shelburne granite, which perhaps was carried off to sea in long past ages, on an iceberg detached from the coast glacier of Nova Scotia, and deposited where we had found it, to be again recovered after such a lapse of time, and to help the solution of the glacial theory, according to which, at one time, ice held Nova Scotia in as close an embrace as it does Iceland and Greenland at the present.

"The weather had not been of the best; cold winds, with occasional snow and rain, greeted us during the time at our disposal here; yet we would fain have made a longer stay amongst such kind friends, of whom it is a pleasure to speak. There was a goodness and cordiality with their hospitality and warmheartedness that can never be forgotten by those who knew them.

"On the 19th May, we steamed out of the harbour, and before nightfall the coast was out of sight."

Of all Shephard's paintings, this one is a veritable enigma. Not only is there no area known as the "Gulf of Florida" on the run from Halifax to Bermuda, her next port of call, but there is no indication in the written records of a storm of the intensity indicated in Shephard's painting.

If Shephard's date of May 21st is correct, the *Challenger* was only two days out of Halifax, at the most some 200 miles along the due south course for Bermuda. There is no "Gulf of Florida" there. Although the Gulf of Mexico was sometimes referred to as the "Gulf of Florida" in the 17th century, a check of 19th Century charts showed no such name in the area between Halifax and Bermuda. Further checks with the Library of Congress did not turn up any reference to a "Gulf of Florida" in this area. The strongest winds on this generally smooth leg of the Expedition were encountered on the 24th and 25th of May (Thomson and Murray, Vol. 1, p. 158). If it is assumed that Shephard missed the date—again—and that his painting relates to an incident on the 24th or 25th of May, then the *Challenger* was five or six days along on a trip of just under 900 miles that took nine days (May 19 to 28). This would put her average speed of advance at 100 miles per day, and on the 24th or 25th she would have been some 500 to 600 miles south of Halifax and 300 to 400 miles north of Bermuda. The temperature section observed by the *Challenger* between Halifax and Bermuda on this leg (Spry, facing p. 68) indicates that the ship would have been in the Gulf Stream—or as the plot of the section indicates it, "delta of the Gulf Stream"—on the 24th and 25th of May. Since Shephard evidently listened to his shipmates as a source for his information (e.g., *"Baruner"* for *Varuna*) it is possible that the "Gulf of Florida" reference might be his interpretation of the talk he had heard aboard about the Gulf Stream coming from Florida or the Straits of Florida. Certainly the *Challenger* had been in the Gulf Stream several

times by mid-May of 1873, and it is just possible that Shephard had associated the "Gulf" term with the warm waters that had a Florida origin. At any rate, it seems to be a complete error of terminology.

The fact of the storm itself is also interesting. Neither Lord Campbell nor Spry makes any mention whatever of a storm, or even of the weather, on this leg. Going back to the official narrative of the Expedition, however, two references are found to the weather on the Halifax-to-Bermuda run (Thomson and Murray, pp. 158 and 159): "On the 19th of May at 5 P.M. the Expedition left Halifax for Bermuda, and fine weather was experienced on the passage. The wind on one occasion only exceeding a force of 5, viz., on the 24th and 25th, on which days a moderate gale was experienced from the S.W., lasting 26 hours". And again (p. 159): "Unfortunately, the weather the 24th was unfavorable either for sounding or dredging, so that it was impossible to test the current by mooring a boat."

The painting, however, is a magnificent one of the *Challenger* in a gale, and it is hardly fair to ask the artist also to be accurate in such minor details as when it happened, where it was, or to stick to the recorded intensity of the storm. This was the first rough weather the *Challenger* had encountered, and it is possible that Shephard was experiencing his first bit of this aspect of life at sea. As most oceanographers know, your first rough-weather experience can be traumatic. Where you are or what day it is becomes magnificently unimportant, and the severity of the storm is always considerably greater as you recount the incident and your own misery later on. Rather than berate him for his minor inaccuracies, we should instead see in them a true reflection of the effects the sea can have on a man, and consider the painting the more accurate because of this note of marine reality.

Shephard did not record the second stop at Bermuda nor the brief anchoring off the island of Fayal in the Azores. They left Fayal upon hearing that there was an epidemic of smallpox, and as Spry reports it (p. 80): ". . . it was deemed prudent not to land, and therefore on the next day proceeded for St. Michael's, which was reached on the 4th; finding it healthy, it was determined to remain for a few days."

Lord Campbell provides the better description of the view shown in Shephard's painting of St. Michael's or "St. Michall" as Shephard calls it (pp. 25-26): "On the 4th we arrived at St. Michael's, having dredged on the way in 900 fms., and got a few starfish and a large dead crinoid. Crinoids being one of the most rare and wished-for things, we dredged again in hopes of more, but unsuccessfully. We have scarcely got one crinoid the whole time we have been away, which disappoints and dismays science.

"The characteristic features of all these islands are much the same, the land sloping from steep sea-cliffs to high volcanic ridges, and every inch of ground apparently cultivated. Ponta Delgardo, the capital of the group and seat of government, is a long white town, of which windows are the principal feature, with a background of rugged low hills extending away to right and left. On the right are some higher and distant hills. To our great joy we found that there was no small-pox here, so we overran the island in all directions. The town is particularly clean, and dull; the corners of every white or yellow house and of every window edged in black. There is a modest but good little hotel kept by an Englishman. St. Michael's is a beautiful island, and it is a wonder that it is not more visited than it is."

The *Challenger* stayed at St. Michael's for five days. "We left St. Michael's on the evening of July the 9th, sounding every day and dredging twice on the way, and anchored off Madeira on the 16th; there we found small-pox very bad, and so, without going on shore, we left next day in the evening for the Cape de Verde Islands." (Campbell, p. 33)

Both Spry and Lord Campbell paint bleak pictures of St. Vincent, but the latter's seems to be done with such loathing that it is worth recording just to prove that every island that oceanographic expeditions touch is not a Tahiti or a Moorea.

"On the 27th we arrived at St. Vincent—one of the Cape de Verde group. St. Vincent is, I think, the most dismal place that I know. The only thing to be said in its favour is that it has a good harbour, in which, for a long time now, a coaling station has been established by an English firm, who have the entire monopoly of coaling the constantly passing mail-steamers and men-of-war. On shore it is simply the abomination of desolation, scarcely a green twig or blade to be seen over miles of barren valley-plains of lava, covered with thin black bushes, scoriae, stones, and rocks, varied occasionally by the corpses of donkeys, or goats, and running between tossed about mountains made of the same materials. Here and there, however, you may come upon a group of tamarisk trees—haunted by insects; now and then you may see a small bird hopping on the ground, or a crow flying by overhead, its harsh cry startling the silence of the burnt-up desert; beneath the stones black geckos hide their ugly forms; and a quail or two *may* rise from the bushes, and reward (?) your day-long search after sport. The population is composed of negroes, a Portugese official or two, two Englishmen connected with the coaling depot, and a few Portugese outlaws—murderers, forgers, *et hoc genus omne*. who, as long as they behave decently, can do as they like.

"The one amusement is to ride donkeys and wretched horses, and as we sailors can make good fun out of even the barrenest lands, when happily we land there, so we got a certain amount of fun from these rides. It is useless to try to walk, the heat is stifling, there is no water, no shade, and your steps are always ankle-deep in sand." (Campbell, pp. 33-34)

11 *"H.M.S. CHALLENGER at St. Vincent & H.M. Troopship SIMOON Leaving fore the Gold-Coast with Marines, July 30, 1873"*

The *Challenger* was at St. Vincent for nine days, and although Spry's account reflects the desolation described by Lord Campbell, the former appears much less dejected by it all, and provides the only description of the town before which Shephard shows the *Challenger* at anchor.

"We had found deep water day after day close up to the island of Antonio (Cape de Verde), which was sighted on the 26th; the soundings now got less, and showed that this island was connected by a ridge with St. Vincent, only 52 fathoms of water being found in some places on it. On the morning of July 27th we anchored off Porto Grande, St. Vincent, and remained until the 5th August. During the stay a survey was made of the anchorage, and the vessel filled up with coal.

"What a contrast in the scenery between this place and Madeira! Here are barren rocks, and not the faintest indication of vegetation to be seen in any direction, although its formation, there can be no doubt, is precisely similar.

"The town, if it can be so named, consists of a few straggling houses and the stores of Messrs. Millar and Co., the coal contractors, situated along the shore, while stretching away behind, are several high, rough, and jagged peaks and mountains, affording a fine background for the barren and uninteresting coast scenery. Scarcely any supplies were to be obtained here. We left on the 5th of August, and the next day reached Santiago, another island of the same group. Here we had somewhat better success, and a fair supply of fruit and vegetables was obtained." (Spry, pp. 83-84)

H.M.S. CHALLENGER, AT. St. VINCENT, & H.M. TROOP. SHIP SIMOON, LEAVING, FORE, THE. GOLD-COAST, WITH, MARINES, JULY 30TH 1873.

The *Challenger's* run from St. Iago in the Cape Verdes south to 3° N and then west to St. Paul's Rocks was a productive one scientifically, and Shephard's painting of her with all sails set seems to reflect the confidence that comes with success. On this leg, they encountered spectacular bioluminescense, and Lord Campbell's description of this always interesting phenomenon is particularly vivid (p. 39):

"On the night of the 14th the sea was most gloriously phosphorescent, to a degree unequalled in our experience. A fresh breeze was blowing, and every wave and wavelet as far as one could see from the ship on all sides to the distant horizon flashed brightly as they broke, while above the horizon hung a faint but visible white light. Astern of the ship, deep down where the keel cut the water, glowed a broad band of blue, emerald-green light, from which came streaming up, or floated on the surface, myriads of yellow sparks, which glittered and sparkled against the brilliant cloud-light below, until both mingled and died out astern far away in our wake. Ahead of the ship, where the old bluff bows of the *Challenger* went ploughing and churning through the sea, there was light enough to read the smallest print with ease. It was as if the 'milky way', as seen through a telescope, 'scattered in millions like glittering dust', had dropped down on the ocean, and we were sailing through it. That is, if you will, a far-fetched comparison, but a more or less true one all the same."

The success of the trawls en route to St. Paul's Rocks enlivened the trip, and again it is Lord Campbell who provides the better description (p. 40):

"We sounded 13 times, dredged once, and trawled 4 times, for we have almost given up the dredge altogether, the trawl proving so much more successful. Fish were always caught, and among them was usually a new species or two. Red shrimps invariably appear, large and small, all of the most crimson-red colour; many of these are quite unknown to science. Twice we have got 'holothurians'—lumps of purple gristle—and starfish, from depths of 2,500 fms.; these, of course, must live at the bottom, but whereabouts the fish and shrimps enjoy their existance is not with any certainty made out, for, of course, the trawl might catch them while sinking or being lifted up at any intermediate depth.

"We have found *all* the foraminiferae, which science (young as yet in these matters) said lived at, and only at the bottom, alive at small depths below the surface, and sometimes on the surface. A towing-net sunk to 50 fms, will come up teeming with small crustaceans, foraminiferae, &c., when there is nothing on the actual surface.

"A trawling at 1,800 fms. resulted in several starfish; two fish, one small kind having a thin membrane of skin covering the eyes, the other a new and most hideous species of mudfish; a number of crimson shrimps; an *umbellularia*, the fourth one we have now found, but not a very fine specimen; a crinoid; a sea-urchin with long spines; worms, new and very rare, &c.

"The Professor, having previously made a bet with the mess generally that we should not get another *umbellularia*, tonight, at dinner, paid the penalty in champagne 'all round.' The trawl is a fruitful source of innocent betting; we bet each other glasses of sherry and bitters, that no starfish, or no worms, or no sea-urchin comes up, and this stimulates whatever excitement we may have in the day's results."

Actually, oceanographic expeditions and the scientist–crew relationship have changed little since the *Challenger* Expedition —with the one possible exception that champagne does not normally appear on the provisioning list for today's expeditions. Shephard's painting reflects the same feeling of "all's well with the world" that Lord Campbell's narration of this leg conveys.

13   *"H.M.S. CHALLENGER Made Fast to St. Paul's Rocks, AGst 28th, 1873"*

This is one of the best-known illustrations from the *Challenger* Expedition, but the familiar one is by the Expedition Artist, J. J. Wild, and appears as Figure 86 on page 201 of Volume 1 of the Thomson and Murray official narrative of the expedition. There are several explanations. Photographs were taken during the Expedition, and it is possible that both artists worked from the same photograph, for certainly the boats are in the exact position. Even the rocks are the same in both illustrations. Perhaps Wild did the original, and Shephard copied his; or perhaps it was the other way around. In any case, it is a fine painting of the *Challenger* "made fast" to St. Paul's Rocks.

Spry gives only passing comment to this event (p. 86): "On the 27th August land was reported, and as we neared St. Paul's Rocks, so the little pinnacles in the midst of the ocean became clearer and clearer. There was deep water close to; so we secured to the lee-side by means of a large hawser."

Lord Campbell, on the other hand, provided more detail of the tie-up to the rocks (pp. 40-41): "On August the 27th we sighted St. Paul's Rocks, steamed to leeward of them, and as there is no anchorage, sent boats with ropes and hawsers to the rocks, wound a rope round and round a bit of rock, made a hawser fast to that rope, and swung to it with a length of 75 fms. of hawser, 104 fms. of water under our bows, and there we comfortably lay for a day and two nights made fast to a pinnacle of rock in the middle of the Atlantic!—something no other ship has ever done here before."

About the rocks themselves, Spry adds (pp. 86-87): "The rocks are situated in 0° 58′ north latitude, and 29° 15′ west longitude. They are 540 miles from the coast of South America, and 350 from Fernando Noronha. The highest point is only about 60 feet above the level of the sea. In moderately fine weather a landing can usually be effected. Hundreds of sea-birds frequent them; but there is not a single plant or moss to be found, nor any fresh water to be obtained.

"During the two days of our stay the rocks were alive with surveyors, naturalists, and others. Fish was to be obtained in abundance. A thorough geological examination was made, with a view to test the practicability of erecting a lighthouse, as a monument to the memory of the late Captain Maury, United States Navy—who was the father of deep-sea exploration and who has rendered such important aid to navigation. However, from our observations the decision was altogether unfavourable."

Regardless of the origins of this painting, it is a classic in oceanography.

14 *"H.M.S. CHALLENGER Leaving St. Paul's Rocks, AGst 29, 1873"*

This is the standard profile of St. Paul's Rocks as recorded by the *Challenger* Expedition. Again, as with the classic picture of the ship tied up to the rocks, it may have been done from a photograph, or Shephard or Wild may have copied the other's original. At any rate, the identical view of the rocks, but without the *Challenger* in the foreground, appears as the plate facing page 86 in Spry. The one done by Shephard extends farther both to the right and to the left than the Wild version, and the cloud patterns are considerably different, but the rocks are exactly the same where they cover the same area.

The *Challenger* was only 58′ north of the Equator at St. Paul's Rocks, and as she cast off from her mid-Atlantic mooring and headed south, she soon crossed the Line. It is interesting that no observance of the entrance into the realm of Neptunus Rex was allowed, and it is even more interesting that the rest of the expedition went well without the ship's having made the mandatory reverence to the king of the deep. Although Spry commented that the practice of holding appropriate ceremonies on crossing the Equator was falling into disuse, today's oceanographers have revived the ancient rite, and no research ship now dares cross the Line without appro-priate ceremonies honoring Neptunus Rex. Spry tells of the departure from St. Paul's Rocks which Shephard painted thusly (p. 87):

"On the morning of 29th August hawsers were cast off, and we steamed round the rocks, taking soundings and current observations; and then on the next day crossed the Equator in longitude 30° 18′ west. The disagreeable practice of shaving, &c., those who for the first time 'cross the line' was not permitted, although there were many who were anxious to join in the usual sport. This old-fashioned custom, which the present age seems inclined to get rid of, is gradually falling into disuse, and but few ships' companies now pay that homage on entering Neptune's dominions as were wont to. So the invisible belt was crossed; and as the night advanced the more striking became the aspect of the Southern Constellations. The sparkling light of the North Star had for some time past been growing fainter, and at length disappeared altogether. On the other hand, the Southern Cross, and other stars with which we were not so familiar, had taken their places; and each night, as we moved farther south, for a time we felt a difficulty in recognising our new acquaintances."

15 *"H.M.S. CHALLENGER Leaving Fanando de Noronah, Sept. 3d, 1873"*

The *Challenger* arrived at the Brazilian island of Fernando Noronha on September 1st, 1873. Even as today's oceanographic expeditions occasionally are refused permission to work in the waters of another country, the *Challenger* was not allowed to survey in the waters surrounding the island or even to collect biological specimens from the island itself. Campbell reports the incident this way (p. 45):

"On Sept. the 1st we arrived at Fernando Noronha, a pretty green little island from whose wooded hills shoot here and there grey pinnacles of rock. One of these in particular is of curious shape and a thousand feet high. The island belongs to Brazil, and is used as a convict settlement, there being now thirteen hundred convicts, who live in little wooden huts, which, with barracks for two hundred soldiers, prisons, and an ancient fort, make up the cheery settlement. The Governor, on being visited by the Captain, appeared to be much puzzled by us. 'Was that the English flag? Were we a man-of-war?' and other curious questions. He was evidently confused and perturbed in spirit because we did not salute, and our explanation that we had only two guns, produced all the more confusion as to how we *could* be a man-of-war. However, he was very civil, gave us leave to do what we liked, and offered to lend us horses. But next morning he had changed his mind, would allow no survey to be carried on, even refusing leave for the naturalists or anybody else to rummage the island in search of butterflies, beetles, and plants! What sinister motive was ascribed to us this Brazilian governor alone can say, for officers from other ships have never been vetoed before. So, as there was nothing to be done, we left in dudgeon, of which I was mighty glad, as it was a stupid little place, and the original intention had been to stay there ten days or so."

Shephard's odd-shaped pinnacle at the right in the painting is in fact an accurate representation of the 1000-foot peak called the Pyramid. This is the peak with the "curious shape" mentioned in Campbell's account of the visit. The *Challenger* in the painting appears to be dredging under power, although neither the Spry nor the Campbell account mentions this operation. They did, however, dredge inshore from the pinnace and evidently decided to do some surveying in spite of the governor's refusal to grant permission, for Campbell (p. 46) tells of a landing on one of the small islets: "The landing was not easy, and one of our boats was capsized in the surf—sextants, theodolites, watches, officers, and men, all tumbling into the water." One does not take theodolites and sextants in a small boat unless a survey is planned. Although unrecorded, the Captain must have decided "The Governor be hanged, we'll survey anyway".

Twenty days after leaving Bahia, Brazil, the *Challenger* arrived at Tristan de Cunha in the mid-South Atlantic on October 15th, even though Shephard's title says the 14th. They were well along on their trans-Atlantic profile, and it had been a good run down from Bahia. This painting is the only one showing dolphins playing ahead of the ship, and they may reflect the general feeling of pleasurable comfort now that the ship was in cooler latitudes.

"A section was now commenced across the Atlantic to the Cape of Good Hope. When clear of the land (Brazil, ed.), sail was made, and with a pleasant breeze, we raced on into cooler and healthier latitudes. It had been intended to sight and make a short stay off the little island of Trinidad, a rocky and barren spot, surrounded with a dangerous shore of almost unapproachable, sharp, rugged rock, over which generally a rough and turbulent surf breaks, affording security to innumerable seabirds, for whose refuge it seems expressly formed.

"Owing, however, to unfavourable winds and other causes, we were unable to get nearer than 300 miles; so our course was altered for Tristan d'Acunha. During the passage the usual programme of sounding and trawling was carried out when opportunities offered. The ocean seems teeming with animated organisms. The drift nets, which are always trailing behind us, get filled in a short time with immense numbers of little lively creatures, pretty-looking red and blue cockles, sea-nettle, and various other inhabitants of the deep, many of the most minute size and delicate form and tint.

"In the work-room was disclosed, by aid of the microscope, to the observer, an entirely new world in the economy of nature as displayed in the animal life from the surface of the sea.

"On the 6th October, in lat. 30° south, we picked up the commencement of the 'westerlies', and by their influence we made short work of the 900 miles still separating us from the islands. On the morning of the 15th land was in sight, a little speck at first rising up dark and rugged out of the sea, growing larger and larger as we neared, terminating at length in a huge conical peak some 8000 feet in height covered with snow." (Spry, pp. 92-94)

After some 20 days at sea, the magnificent snow-capped peak of Tristan de Cunha must have been a welcome sight, and Shephard has done it justice in this fine painting of the island.

"Anchorage is on the north side of the island, and a mighty bad one it is. A precipitous wall of cliff, rising abruptly from the sea, encircles the island, excepting where the settlement is, and there the cliff recedes and leaves a long grass slope of considerable extent covered with grey boulders. On this slope are built the cottages, which look very Scotch from the ship, with their white walls—built of large blocks of stone well cut and dove-tailed together—straw roofs, and dykes around them. Sheep, cattle, pigs, geese, ducks, and fowls they have in plenty, also potatoes and other vegetables, all of which they sell to whalers, who give them flour or money in exchange.

"The appearance of the place makes one shudder; it looks so thoroughly as though it were always blowing there, which indeed it is, heavy storms continually sweeping over, killing their cattle right and left before they have time to drive them under shelter." (Campbell, p. 61)

Spry (pp. 94-95) adds to the accounts of the small windy settlement depicted by Shephard: "At the time of our visit the population consisted of some twenty families, numbering eighty-four in all. Soon after our anchoring a boat came off with seventeen of the islanders. Amongst them was Peter Green, their governor, from whom it was ascertained that they had plenty of cattle and vegetables for sale. This was welcome news, for fresh provisions are always acceptable after being a long time at sea. They however proved, as was found out later, that they were not above trying to make a good bargain out of us, and consequently spoiled the market for themselves.

"We had approached the land as near as safety permitted; the weather promising to be fine, opportunities were taken to land. Soon after leaving the vessel, an extensive belt of sea-weed was found encircling the island, forming a natural breakwater, and so preventing the violence of the heavy Atlantic surf breaking, as it otherwise would, along the shore.

"Before reaching the land, all, more or less, got a wetting, as the rollers break along the beach, but after a scramble all landed right enough, and made a tour of the settlement, which is named Edinburg, in compliment to Prince Alfred, who visited here in 1867, when in command of the GALATEA.

"About fifteen houses are seen scattered over an open space on the north side of the island. There are several enclosures where potatoes and other vegetables are grown, and the islanders possess, in common, some four or five hundred head of cattle and a plentiful supply of poultry and pigs.

"As the day advanced, the weather changed to wind and rain, and it was with some difficulty all got on board in safety."

H.M.S. CHALLENGER. AT TRISTAN.DE.CUNHA.OCT 14TH 1873.

18 *"H.M.S. CHALLENGER visit to Inaccessible Island, Oct. 16th 1873 & takeing two abonded men away setting fire to their dwelling"*

The two men mentioned in the title of Shephard's painting of Inaccessible Island were Frederick Stoltenhoff and his younger brother, Gustav. They were not abandoned or "abonded" as Shephard spells it, but had settled there some two years before. They had taken passage aboard the New Bedford whaler, *Java*, under Captain Manter, at St. Helena and planned to settle on Tristan de Cunha. During the passage, Captain Manter painted such a dreary picture of Tristan and its inhabitants and such a glowing one of uninhabited Inaccessible, that they changed their minds and landed on the latter. The full story of their futile attempt to hunt seals for profit and the hardships they endured was narrated to the *Challenger's* Paymaster, one R. R. Richards, and is presented in full by Spry (pp. 96-109).

Campbell gives an account of the incident depicted by Shephard (pp. 62-63 and 66): "They told us of two Germans who were put on an island fifteen miles from here, some time ago; and as they have not been over there or seen any signs of them for a long time, they fear they are ill or dead. So that evening we got under way, being hurried off by dirty-looking weather and a squall from the N. W. Before going we took in abundant and welcome supplies of beef, sheep, fowls, pigs, and potatoes for all hands. We steamed slowly over during the night, and early next morning anchored off the northern side of Inaccessible Island: a magnificent wall of black cliff, splashed green with moss and ferns, rising sheer 1,300 feet above the sea, and beneath it a strip of stony beach, about a mile in length, stretching between two bold bluffs. At the foot of the cliffs we saw a hut, and soon afterwards the two Germans; very good fellows they proved to be, talking capital English, and delighted to see us; we gave them passage to the Cape. . . . In the afternoon the ship steamed round the island, sounding, dredging, and taking a running survey, which had not been done before. Bold cliffs encircle it, but in some parts are not so high as those on the north side, and there it is quite practical to get up them. That night we again anchored in the same place, the Germans coming off with their traps, first, however, burning their hut, so that the Tristan people, to whom they bear no good will, may not benefit by it in any of their seal-hunting excursions."

On arrival at the Cape of Good Hope on October 28th, 1873, the younger of the Stoltenhoff brothers left the *Challenger* and immediately headed for home, while the elder obtained a position as a clerk in a local business house and remained at Capetown.

"Under way the next morning, we steamed in a few hours over to Nightingale Island, the remaining island of the group; the continued fine weather tempting us to explore these hitherto unvisited islands, this small one being only marked with a dotted line on the chart. . . . The island looked charming from the sea, being apparently beautifully grassed, with bushes growing in the gullies. But what was our disappointment to find on closer acquaintance that the whole island was in reality covered with tall tussock grass, which concealed enormous rookeries of penguins!" (Campbell, p. 66)

However, the birds on the rocks in the foreground of Shephard's painting are apparently mollymawks, for they also abounded on these rocks at the time of the *Challenger* visit. Drawing No. 26 shows that Shephard could paint passable penguins, so these must be the mollymawks that Campbell described from Nightingale Island (p. 66-67): "They are beautiful birds, snow-white throat and breast, black wings and tail, back of the head and neck tinted a pearly grey, a black bill with an orange streak on the upper mandible, black eyes under a straight black eyebrow, which, with a soft dark edging around the eye, gives them an odd look of half fierceness, half gentleness . . . looking quietly dignified as they walked or sat on their high nests among the squatting, screaming penguins."

It was the penguins, however, that made the visit to Nightingale a memorable one for men of the *Challenger*, and Campbell's version of the shore visit is a graphic one (p. 70):

"The grass grew six feet high, matted and tangled, while thousands of penguins swarmed between the tufted stems. If ever we stopped to see where we placed our feet, instantly we were attacked by a host of infuriated harpies . . You can have no conception how infuriated and bold they are when protecting their nests, rushing at our legs in crowds, and following us pecking viciously. They were so thick that it was useless trying to avoid them, so one just had to tramp on as fast as possible, striking out forward and sideways vigorously, every step knocking down, kicking, and treading on an india-rubbery substance, which if you dare to look down you will find is a penguin, or smash, smash, as you tread on eggs by the dozen; or—more dreadful still—squash, squash, as you tread on the small black creatures—horrible! horrible! But being a truthful narrator, I must chronicle these dreadful facts: add to all this the slippery dirty ground (it all reminded me of that line, 'The slithy toves did gyre and gimble in the wabe'), the furies biting hard incessantly—reaching not only that inch of stocking between gaiters and knickerbockers, but higher up, too, as I sunk into a hollow or hole,—the deafening brayings, the overpowering stench, the clouds of small black flies, which if one opened one's mouth was bound to swallow *en masse*, the hard work fighting, rifle in hand, through the matted grass, the not being able to see where one was going, or when it would all end, till suddenly we were stopped by finding ourselves on the brink of a low cliff, and uncommonly nearly over it we were too, but oh, joy! . . . it was like escaping from the regions of the—you know!"

"H.M.S. CHALLENGER arrive at Simons Bay, Cape of Good Hope, Oct. 28th, 1873"

The ten-day run from Nightingale Island to the Cape of Good Hope was one of heavy weather, and few soundings were made. Those obtained, however, did show that there was a deeper "channel" by some 600 fathoms on the east than they had encountered on the run from Brazil to Tristan on the first half of their trans-Atlantic profile.

"On the 28th October the land was reported, and soon the famous Table Mountain of the Cape was visible from the deck; the thirty-three days of our passage had now seemingly quickly passed, and we were still able to easily recall the many incidents at Bahia, and the varied scenes occurring in the 3000 miles just traversed over.

"And now as we near the African shore, with its outline of peculiar shape, our hopes and thoughts fly back to other lands, on the one hand thankful for successes so far, and on the other full of hope for the future. It was late in the day before we were fairly in for sounding; serials and current observations had to be taken off the Cape of Storms. Therefore it was about 4 P.M. when we anchored in Simon's Bay, within half a mile of the shore, where Simon's Town is situated. In consequence of the case of yellow fever while at Bahia, two days' quarantine was imposed, after which all were free for a run on shore." (Spry, pp. 109-10)

It had been a long crossing, and as Spry's "hopes and thoughts fly back to other lands", one suspects that even the men on the *Challenger* got occasional touches of what today's oceanographers call "channel fever" as land approaches. The scene painted by Shephard both in this sketch and in its near duplicate in No. 22, is nicely described by Spry (p. 112):

"There can scarcely be a landscape more gloomy and desolate than the sterile rocky mountain and white sandy plains which inclose Simon's Bay. Coming from the coast of Brazil, the beautiful garden scenery of St. Michael's, with its luxuriant verdure, the contrast becomes doubly unpleasing and cheerless. The town consists of about a couple of hundred of square white-washed houses, which are scattered along the beach, with scarcely a single tree in the neighbourhood for shelter, backed up with lofty, steep, bare hills of sandstone. The Naval Yard occupies a prominent position, and is of great service to the vessels employed on this station; here repairs are efficiently performed, and stores of all descriptions are to be obtained.

"The Naval Hospital is a capital airy and well-ventilated establishment; this, together with the residence of the Commodore, and two or three churches and chapels, constitutes all the buildings with any pretensions to size."

In this painting the *Challenger* is the ship in the right background shown entering the bay.

During the stop at Simon's Bay, the men of the *Challenger* roamed over the countryside. From Simon's Town they explored wherever the roads led them. They visited the fishing hamlet of Cork Bay, the vineyards of Constantia, and on to Wynberg and even Cape Town itself. In late November the *Challenger* moved from Simon's Bay to Table Bay.

"After completing stores, and having refitted ship, we steamed round the famous Cape of Storms for Table Bay. The forty miles run was soon accomplished, and the anchors let go about a couple of miles from shore. It was intended we should have gone in the dock basin, so as to have given the inhabitants of the town free run on board, but the dock master was afraid of our size, and the damage we might probably have caused to his jetty and bollards, if a south-easter should come on, which seemed very likely at this season; so we had to be visited at this distance, with all the inconveniences of again reaching shore.

"A ball was given during our stay in the Commercial Build-ings. Our guests told us that nothing so perfect and complete had ever been held before. Concerning the decorations, they were particularly enthusiastic, for there were, as novelties, trophies of dredging and sounding apparatus, with flags, flowers, and evergreens, giving certainly a very pleasing effect. Suffice it to say, all passed off most agreeably. The following night the citizens of Cape Town gave a return ball in the same building, when everything was done by them to insure success, and, without any flattery, nothing could have exceeded the completeness of the arrangements or the hospitality of the givers." (Spry, pp. 117-8)

Shephard has shown the *Challenger* anchored with both anchors, and her two anchor buoys show clearly off the bow. The view of Table Mountain is a classic one, but the so-called "tablecloth" of clouds that often covers it is absent, and the full profile of the mountain is shown.

This painting is in many respects identical to No. 20. There are some differences in the background hills, but the town to the right and even the British man-of-war are almost identical to those in the earlier painting. It is interesting to note that the wind is blowing in the opposite direction from that in the earlier painting, and all flags are now flying towards the left. The *Challenger*, at the right, is close onto the lee shore and from the appearance of the sails on her foremast is apparently "backing down" preparatory to clearing the harbor and heading again for sea.

"The next day the ship was swung in the Bay (Table Bay, ed.) for magnetic corrections, after which we proceeded to Simon's Bay to complete stores and refitment. This was finished by the 16th December, and the next day we steamed out of Simon's Bay for our Antarctic cruise.

"The weather was beautifully fine, and as Cape Point was passed, and the high land of the Table Mountains receded from our sight, a southerly course was shaped; and on the 19th, 80 miles to the southward of the Cape, we entered the Agulhas current, the breadth of which was found to be about 250 miles, and the temperature of the surrounding sea was influenced to a depth of at least 400 fathoms. It was intended to have made a close examination of this enormous body of heated water, which is derived from similar sources as the Gulf Stream of the Atlantic, and exercises such great influence on the climate of the Cape and its adjacent seas.

"The heated water of the Indian Ocean, forced to the westward by the north-east monsoon and south-east trade-winds, has only one outlet, the sea south of the Cape. On arriving there, it is met, and stopped, by the cold Atlantic easterly drift current, produced by the continuous westerly winds of the higher latitudes, which is sufficiently powerful to turn it aside and absorb it. It is then driven to the south-east and eastward, the two bodies of water intermixing. This drift also prevents any branch of the warm current passing to the northward round the Cape.

"The strong winds now met with prevented a closer examination, but from the observations made it appears that the water in Table Bay, derived from the South Atlantic, is usually 10° colder than that in Simon's Bay, 30 miles to the southward, which is derived from the Indian Ocean. But on the approach of a north-west wind the Atlantic water drives the Indian water out of Simon's Bay, and occupies its place. Thus the water in the bay is liable to sudden changes of temperature to the extent of 10° or 12°." (Spry, pp. 118-119)

Shephard is occasionally off on his dates, often off on his spelling, but seldom off on his islands. In the case of this painting, however, he is most probably painting the landing at Marion Island on December 26th, 1873. No landing was attempted on nearby Prince Edward Island. Spry (p. 121) tells of the situation this way: "It was intended, on the following day (December 27th, ed.), to land on Prince Edward Island, but from the unfavourable appearance of the weather the idea was reluctantly given up." Campbell's account is essentially the same (p. 88): "Dec. 27—Knocking about between the islands last night, and dredging all day. We have given up going to Prince Edward's Island on account of the weather being misty."

On December 26th, however, they did come in close to Marion Island and put out a boat to investigate the possibility of a landing. The fact that there is a boat over in Shephard's painting and that the date is December 26th strongly suggests the painting is of Marion rather than Prince Edward Island.

As a sidelight, it is interesting to note that this is the second Christmas Day that the *Challenger* has spent at sea. Today's oceanographic vessels have a great penchant for being either at home or at some friendly port over Christmas. Christmas of 1872 was spent in the English Channel some four days out of Portsmouth, and Christmas of 1873 was passed off Marion Island at some 48° south.

Assuming that this painting is in fact of Marion rather than of Prince Edward Island which they bypassed on the 27th, Campbell describes the island and the landing thus (pp. 83-84):

"Dec. 26.—A beautiful sunny morning. Steamed close up to leeward of Marion Island. A rock-bound shore edging a long green slope rising gradually up to about 3,000 feet; the mountain peaks hid in white clouds and mist, and snow lying to about half-way down; numbers of small crater cones cropping up here and there from shore to summit, some of the most vivid red colour; rounded streams of grass-covered lava, broken off in places in high, black precipices; shadows of clouds flitting over the sunlit mottled green slopes of the lower land; sunshine lighting up the snow on the higher peaks, and the patches lying on the black rocks in the middle distance. With the naked eye we could see large white objects all over the lower land, which in a civilized country might have been very white sheep, but here, with our glasses, we could see they were albatross sitting on their nests, while numbers were flying round us and settling on the water, where, too, flocks of penguins and shags were swimming and diving.

"After sending a boat in to discover whether landing was practicable, we landed on the rocks in a small cove, which with care was tolerably easy, the day being particularly fine and calm, and an outlying belt of kelp smoothing the water; but if it had been a rough day we should not have been able to land here at all."

The date, the longboat pulling in to the rocky shore, and the "Shadows of clouds flitting over the sunlit mottled green slopes of the lower land" all support the contention that Shephard's painting is of Marion Island.

The Crozets are a grim group of islands at about 45° South in the southwestern Indian Ocean, and the *Challenger* moved in close among them but was unable to effect a landing because of the bad weather. Shephard's painting reflects the abundance of birds seen but shows little of the misty and foggy weather encountered during the short time the ship was in this group of islands.

"On the 31st of December, after a succession of strong north-westerly winds, the first of the Crozet group of islands was seen; but the weather prevented any hope which might have been indulged in of effecting a landing; however, the islands, six in number, were all seen, and their correct position ascertained. It is over one hundred years ago that they were discovered and reported. Possessing no interest in a geographical point of view, and having no resources, they are therefore more to be avoided than approached. Very little is known about them, for Sir J. C. Ross's expedition was unable to land in 1843, and now the *Challenger's* was equally unfortunate. Later in the day the lofty mountain of East Island was seen through the haze, and on it clearing we had a good view of this perfect mountain mass of volcanic land, with its bold and precipitous shores and projecting rocks, which seem to have been formed by the unceasing action of the waves cutting away the softer parts. We stood up between the channel separating East and Possession Islands, the largest of the group, but saw no indication of tree or shrub. It was intended to make a short stay in America Bay, but the strong north-west wind prevented our reaching it before dark, and encountering a heavy cross sea, it was not considered safe to venture nearer. A dense fog now setting in, and a heavy gale of wind springing up, it was evident we were to be disappointed; so we stood off to sea, and the opportunity of again closing the land was not afforded." (Spry, pp. 122-123)

25 "H.M.S. CHALLENGER visit to Royal Sound, Kerguelen Island, Jan., 1874"

This is one of the Shephard paintings that very clearly shows the *Challenger's* stack. The small vessel at the left is an American sealing schooner, and in the foreground the *Challenger's* longboat is pulling in for a landing on Kerguelen. This island had already seen the boats of many expeditions. Cook had been there in 1777. The Frenchman, Kerguelen, on an exploring expedition in 1772 first landed there, and Sir James Ross anchored his *Erebus* and *Terror* in Christmas Harbor (see No. 26) in 1840.

Kerguelen has numerous excellent harbors, of which Royal Sound is the deepest on the south coast. Campbell provides a description of the *Challenger's* visit there (pp. 99-100):

"On the morning of Jan. the 16th, we left Betsy Cove, getting a good blow that night, and the next morning steered along a low grass-covered land, dotted white with Albatross sitting on their nests, and large penguin rookeries at frequent intervals along the shore. While the ship stopped and dredged, a boat landed under a high foreland, where we saw two more sea-elephants, and shot a great many ducks, and then we steamed up Royal Sound. A magnificent sound, running many miles into the land the upper end crowded with small islands, among which we anchored in the evening, finding a sealing schooner at anchor, this being their head-quarters. To the north and west are fine mountain ranges, the western shore of the sound being lined with a volcanic line of high conical hills. Next day we had some capital duck-shooting, steaming farther up the sound in our steam pinnace; a bright sun, water smooth as a mill-pond, and studded with small green islands—quite lovely!"

Meeting another ship in such a remote spot was an occasion for a visit, and Campbell recorded some of the conversation (p. 100):

"The captain of this sealing schooner was a regular Yankee character. 'Guessed we were out of our reckoning, and how on airth did we find our way in here?' It being explained that we were a 'discovery ship', he 'guessed there was another island down south we could go and discover!' (meaning Head Island—this was sarcasm.) Asked if he would dine and come to church on Sunday, he 'guessed he had not been to church for fourteen years, and did not think he would commence again now'."

Christmas Harbor on Kerguelen was named by Captain Cook when he anchored the *Discovery* and *Resolution* there on Christmas Day in 1777. This painting of the *Challenger* in Christmas Harbor is one of Shephard's most delightful ones, and the abundance of birds he shows is evidently no exaggeration. Spry states (pp. 128-9):

"The number of birds found here is surprising. Although I had often heard of the great numbers met with on uninhabited islands, I was scarcely prepared to see them in such vast multitudes, particularly the penguins, for the whole sides of the rugged hills and ledges of rocks were literally covered with them. They averaged from 10 to 20 inches in height, with white breasts and nearly black backs. The king bird and another species have four or five yellow feathers, from 3 to 5 inches long, adorning each side of their heads in graceful plumes. They stand erect in rows, which gives them a novel and curious appearance; and the noise from these rookeries was deafening. Besides these birds, we were enabled to secure specimens of twenty other varieties."

During her stay at Kerguelen, the *Challenger* made at least two visits to this most interesting harbor, the first on January 7th is depicted by Shephard. Campbell records the scene as they arrived (pp. 90-91):

"Jan 7 (Christmas Harbour).—Got in here at nine o'clock this morning—the 'land of desolation' as old Cook called it, and as it is still called by the sealers. Kerguelen's Island *is* a gloomy-looking island certainly, with its high, black, fringing cliffs, patches of snow on the higher reaches of the dark-coloured mountains, and a grey sea, fretted with white horses, surrounding it. To right and left of the harbour's entrance are perpendicular, table-topped, lava cliffs, covered on the top with green moss. On the left an oblong-shaped block of cliff is separated by a deep cut from the neighboring cliff, of which it once formed a part; in this detached bit is a colossal arch, 150 feet in height, and 100 feet across at the base—a grand freak of nature. The harbour narrows to 500 yards some distance from its head, towards which it gradually tapers, ending in a sandy beach. As we lie at anchor, on our left, towering 1,000 feet above us, is an enormous rounded mass of black basalt, which has burst through rock of older formation and there remained. On our right is a steep slope, covered with moss and grass, traversed occasionally by horizontal banks of trap-rock, and capped by a peak of grey rock—an old crater—1,300 feet high. Ahead, rising from the beach, the mossy slope continues, while beyond, and right and left, are bare brown hills."

Campbell tells of the last day of their final visit to this harbor on January 30th, 1874 (pp. 103-104): "We remained the next day in Christmas Harbour, and a party went away in a boat to the arched rock to see a vein of brown coal which runs between two layers of basalt a few feet above the sea near there; it is very poor stuff, and our men could make nothing of it in a fire. But how different must have been the climate of this land ages ago! The sealers tell us that there is some more of this coal in another place, but they do not make any use of it.

"Jan. 31.—Good-bye to Kerguelen's to-day, having left in a cairn sealed-up copies of the harbours we have surveyed for the Transit people when they come. I have enjoyed the 'Land of Desolation' altogether very much; no bad weather as Ross had—at least not in harbour."

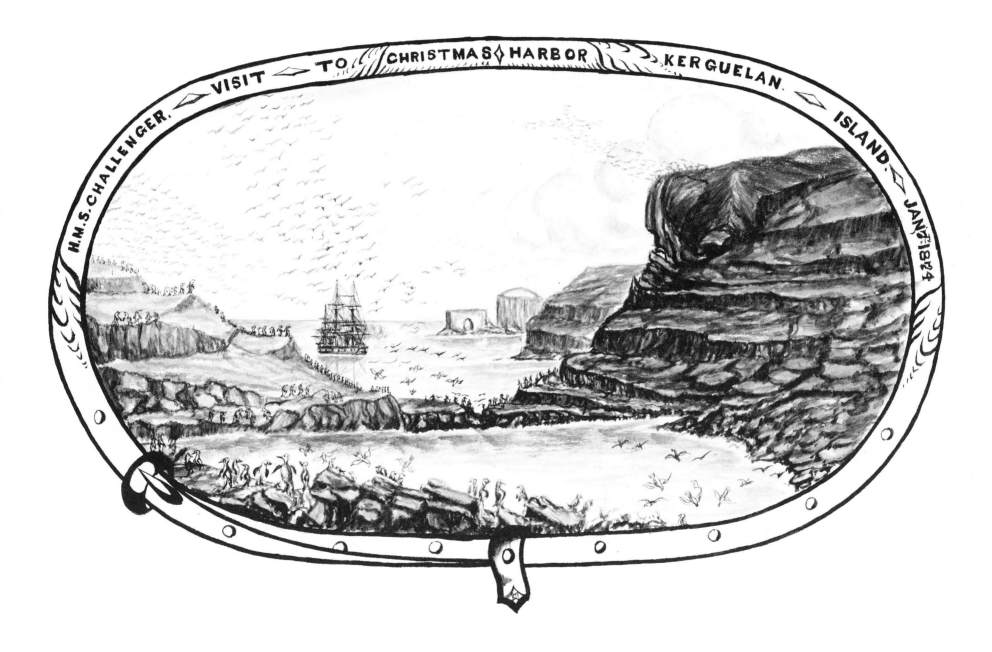

Shephard did three fine paintings of the *Challenger* at Kerguelen, and each title has a different spelling of the island's name. This painting has the distinction, however, of also having the wrong date. The *Challenger* left Christmas Harbour on the 31st of January, and it was not until the following day, February 1st, that she reached the southern-most tip of Kerguelen Island, a point which the Expedition named Cape Challenger. These minor inaccuracies of date and spelling are, however, magnificently unimportant, for the painting itself is a beauty. Shephard shows the *Challenger* in rough seas and strong winds moving along under only her fore and main topsails, the foresail and mainsail being furled, and the others not in evidence. As earlier suggested by the painting of the ship tied up to Saint Paul's Rocks (No. 12), Shephard and the official expedition artist, J. J. Wild, undoubtedly worked together from time to time. Wild's engraving of the *Challenger* off Cape Challenger appears on page 343 of Volume 1 of the Thomson and Murray official narrative of the expedition. In comparing the two, one is immediately struck by the fact that the peaks of Cape Challenger are exactly the same—every crag and pinnacle is in exactly the same position in both. However, in the Wild version, the *Challenger* is on the opposite tack, and the ship is headed towards the right. From the detailed track chart of the expedition during this particular section (Thomson and Burray, 1885, sheet 21, facing page 337), it would appear that it is Shephard in this case who is right, for the direction in which she is sailing is indeed the course on which she passed Cape Challenger on that stormy afternoon in 1874.

Campbell tells of the passage (p. 105): "Feb. 1.—Steaming and sailing along the south shore to 'fix' the southern point of the island, which having done (calling it Cape Challenger), we made sail and shaped our course for Heard Island. We had a fine view of the southern coast and mountain ranges in the evening, the highest mountain of which was calculated by our surveyors to be 6,180 feet high, and called by us Mount Ross, after Captain Sir John Ross."

This naming of newly-discovered or newly-described geographic features for famous people or for one's friends was as common on the *Challenger* Expedition as it is today on oceanographic expeditions or in Antarctica. For today's oceanographers, however, about the only previously undiscovered features remaining are seamounts, and these are generally given the name of the ship that first found them. However, the far ranging oceanographic ships of today such as the *Vema*, the *Atlantis*, the *Melville*, the *Discoverer*, the *Oceanographer*, the *Researcher*, the *Meteor*, and the *Discovery* discover so many seamounts that personal names are often used, although the Board on Geographic Names prefers that such names be limited to those already dead. The *Challenger*, however, had no such restrictions, and on Kerguelen they named the Wyville Thomson Range after the Chief Scientist of the expedition, Mount Campbell after Sub-Lieutenant Lord George G. Campbell, Aldrich Channel after Lieutenant Pelham Aldrich, the surveyor and magnetics man aboard, and Mount Tizzard after Commander Tizzard who was in charge of the navigation and hydrography. The name of the ship itself was reserved for the southernmost cape on Kerguelen, and it is still known as Cape Challenger.

The *Challenger* was now at something more than 50° south latitude, and at Macdonald (also known as Heard Island) they encountered their first real glacier. Shephard shows it graphically in this painting with the *Challenger*'s boat putting in for the beach. Shephard had a great love of reflections, and in many of his paintings he shows the ship and even the details of its rigging reflected in the sea. Often his painting of the wave conditions indicate a sea that no ship could possibly be reflected on, and this painting is one of those.

Campbell best describes the scene that Shephard painted at Macdonald Island (pp. 105-106):

"Feb. 6.—at noon we sighted Heard Island, and bore away for the anchorage. Blowing hard; tremendous squalls off the land. Anything more gloomy or utterly desolate-looking than the island it would be impossible to imagine. High black mountains, their summits enveloped in mist; great masses of snow lying on their slopes, and glaciers descending every gully and bay nearly into the water; bold black headlands; not a speck of green to be seen anywhere. We anchored in the evening in 'Corinthian Bay', of which the sealers had told us. At its head is a long stretch of black sandy beach, from which on the left rises abruptly an enormous glacier—a mountain of ice all seamed and cracked with deep blue fissures, falling right into the sea, stretching continuously a long way along the coast, and up one thousand feet into the mists, which concealed the mountain tops, where these glaciers all have their birth. On the right of the beach, some way back, is a high double-peaked mountain all covered with snow and ice, excepting where black precipices prevent the snow from resting. On the right of the bay a high, black headland—its steep sides spattered white with the breasts of penguins—juts boldly into the sea, completing the round of utter gloom and desolation.

"The captain and a few others landed; a long, cold pull to the beach, where they got on shore pretty easily, though the sealers had told us we could not possibly do so in any of our shaped boats, on account of the heavy surf almost perpetually breaking there. But this evening there was no swell, the wind being off-shore. Wading a muddy stream which ran across the beach from the foot of the glacier, they found half a dozen wretched sealers living in two miserable huts near the beach, and sunk into the ground for warmth and protection against the fierce winds, so fiercely blowing at the time our party landed that they found it necessary to protect their faces from the clouds of sharp sand which were being frisked about. Their work is to kill and boil down sea-elephants as they land. One man has been here for two years, and is going to stay another! They are left here every year by the schooners, while they are sealing or whaling elsewhere. The beach is strewn with the skeletons of sea-elephants."

This, then, is the bay that Shephard depicted. Spry (p. 131) adds only one other note that bears on this painting: ". . . and eventually reached the anchorage in Corinthian Bay (or Whisky Bay of the whalers, so named from the quantities of that spirit said to be consumed by them on the arrival of their store-ship with supplies for the year). All the places previously visited, however inhospitable, really seemed paradise compared with this wretched mountain of ice rising from a base of black lava cinder."

At this time, neither Shephard nor Spry realized just how much "wretched" ice they would be seeing in the next month.

H.M.S. CHALLENGER. VISIT TO M^c DONAL. ISLAND. FEB^Y 6TH 1874.

Like so many others before and after him, Shephard had trouble with the spelling of "Antarctic". One famous national hydrographic service within the past ten years had to re-do the cover for a new atlas of the region, as they too had misspelled it "Antartic". Shephard, however, learned the correct spelling by the time later that month when he did the caption for painting No. 34. Iceberg, however, remains "ice burgh" throughout.

The *Challenger* sighted her first "ice burgh" on February 11th, 1874, at 60° 30′S. Campbell in his journal records the scene (pp. 108-109):

"We got a good haul of the dredge before the expected gale came on, which it did heavily in the afternoon from the north-west; and a heavy sea that night struck the ship forward, smashing in two ports, much to the enjoyment of the sick who were lying in bed behind them.

"Our destination now is 'Termination Land', marked on charts as a good stretch of coast seen by Wilkes, the commander of the American expedition which explored here 30 years ago, who also describes it, however, as an 'appearance of land.' The four following days we ran 550 miles to the southward, and sighted the first iceberg on the morning of the 11th, in lat. 60° 30′S. It was seen at about five miles' distance as a glimmering patch of white against the night sky, and as daylight dawned and we sailed close by it, we saw it to be a large tabular berg about two-thirds of a mile long and 200 feet in height; the top flat and covered with snow, and the perpendicular sides coloured a whitish green—a magnificent sight, to which afterwards we got accustomed. It being nearly a calm, we trawled in 1,260 fms, with the result of a few shells, stones, shrimps, and annelids. Being on the other side of the berg, now, we saw some low blue caverns worn deeply into its side. While watching it in the afternoon, a cloud of spray was seen to rise against it, and when this subsided we saw great masses of ice, which had then fallen off, floating alongside, while the berg rolled perceptibly. Two others were in sight a long way off, their snow-topped summits and portions of cliff visible above the horizon. In the evening we passed close by a large 'calf;' also some smaller pieces—drift and wash ice."

To the men of the *Challenger*, these great masses of floating ice were a totally new experience and they were fascinated by them. While Shephard painted his "ice burghs", both Campbell and Spry wrote detailed descriptions of "these novel sights".

Spry states (pp. 133-134): "Feb. 11th—This morning at an early hour we encountered the first Antarctic iceberg, bearing E.S.E. to our course. On passing within a few miles, it was from observation considered to be three-fourths of a mile long and 200 feet in height. We are now in latitude 60° 52′ south, longitude 80° 20′ west, dredging and sounding frequently with good results. From this time the icebergs became very numerous, and great was the excitement on board as we passed these novel sights. The rich cobalt blue tints blending into the white of the ice produced a very fine effect. The weather was very fine, and each day now we continued to meet icebergs of all shapes and sizes, some apparently much worn by the sea into cavities and great fissures, as if they were ready to split asunder; others of tabular form, with heavy surf breaking up their perpendicular sides. Sailing on, we pass much loose ice, evidently fragments of broken-up icebergs; and a beautiful white petrel, *Procellaria glacius*, was seen for the first time. From this we were led to believe we were in the vicinity of large masses of ice, for it is known that these birds never wander far from the main pack."

Writing on February 13, 1874, Campbell apparently described the exact berg that Shephard drew in No. 30 (pp. 109-110):

"Feb. 13—We have run 240 miles to the southward since meeting the first iceberg, having in that distance only passed 13, but now they are rapidly becoming more numerous. Sailing along with a fair breeze all day. Passed a very long tabular berg this morning, and this evening close to a high-pinnacled one—quite beautiful! The azure blue of the deep fissures and caverns; the sea rushing up the worn-away cliff in great blue waves, falling back, or pouring over curved knife-edges of ice in a torrent of foam and spray. Wilkes' Land 396 miles off."

It was not until March 4th, 1874, that the *Challenger* would see her last ice berg, but that was still three weeks away; and by mid-February these great ice islands were their constant companions and a continuous source of wonderment to all aboard.

On the day that Shephard painted this scene, Campbell wrote (p. 110):

"Feb. 14—Running slowly along in thick weather last night, we suddenly found ourselves in a sea covered with ice—the edge of a pack—large blocks of loose ice grinding against the ship's side, startling some of us rather in bed. We hauled our wind at once and soon got clear of it. Many bergs close around.

"Daylight revealed the pack ahead, the outside loose ice of which we had run into last night—a white rugged field of ice, stretching along five or six points of the compass, with numbers of huge table-topped bergs rising above it. From the masthead we could see scarcely any clear water among the ice, which to the eastward was densely packed, but not so much to the southward.

"Dredged in 1,675 fms. among the 'stream-ice,' a mile and a half off the edge of the pack, but got next to nothing—a squid and some stones. A lovely sunny afternoon, lighting up the glistening pack, bergs, and small ice spread thickly over the water; penguins leaping, and "wh-a-a-ing" loudly; whales blowing in great numbers, and several kinds of birds flying about.

"To-day, for the first time, we have the 'snow-bird,' a pure white petrel— a most beautiful creature. They always keep near the ice, and if seen when yet no ice is visible, are taken as 'sure sign of ice.' They fly higher than other petrels, of which species another new one—light brown and white—joined us yesterday. Besides these we have the sooty albatross, Cape-pigeons, stormy petrels, prions, stinkers, night-hawks, and the penguins—crested and another—in the sea.

"In the evening we made sail and stood to the westward, following the edge of the pack to see what would become of it. This pack-ice is very annoying, effectually barring our road south, where, this being a totally new field of Antarctic exploration, we might have found new land!"

Shephard would go for several weeks without painting and then would paint madly for several days. The mid-February period in 1874 when the *Challenger* was in the midst of the Antarctic ice evidently was a highly stimulating and exciting experience, and paintings Nos. 29 through 34 were all done in less than two weeks. This one and No. 33 both show the ice caves which Campbell described vividly (p. 111):

"No words of mine can describe the beauty of these huge icebergs—one, which we have just sailed past, had three high caverns penetrating a long way in; another was pierced by a hole through which we could see the horizon; and the wonderful colouring of those blue caverns, of the white cliffs, dashed with pale sea-green, and stratified with thin blue lines veining the semi-transparent wall of ice 200 feet in height! As we slip slowly by at night with a light breeze, we can hear the waves roaring against them ceaselessly, and thundering into the caverns. Showers of small snow falling, and freezing on the decks. This evening 47 large bergs, independently of those in the pack, were in sight from the deck, while the pack extended from south-west to east. A very light southerly wind, and a calm sea. (Lat. 65° 30′ S., long 79° 40′ E.)

Campbell further describes these ice caverns two days later (pp. 113-114):

"Feb. 18—Sighted the pack again this morning ahead and on starboard beam, about 100 miles to the eastward of where we first saw it. We sailed quickly along the edge all forenoon on a smooth sea with a fair breeze, boring through 'stream ice,' great flat cakes of ice which had streamed off the heavier pack. What a sight from the masthead! The rough field of ice stretching away as far as one can see; the great bergs in the pack and open water outside, tabular and pinnacled, deep blue caverns worn away in their lofty sides; and the stream ice—flaking white and thickly the dark sea—through which the ship was rapidly and quietly shoving her way, leaving a broad black lane of water behind her, 'starboard' or 'port' being hailed every minute, to clear some piece too heavy for pleasant bumping. The ice became too heavy at last, so we hauled out of it. At noon we passed the northern point of the pack, which then trended away till lost sight of to the south-east, while we kept on to the east-south-east; 20 bergs in sight in afternoon, and geting rarer as we went on. A very cold, though fine day, temperature 24°. Thick fine snow falling to-night, lying two inches deep. Wind shifted to north-west (Run N. 80° E. 116 miles, lat. 64° 44′ S., long. 83° 26′ E.) . . . In the evening we passed a very high one within a ship's length, in which there was a high arched cavern of the most indescribably lovely colour —no painting could realize it, and if it could, you would not believe its truth; the colour and exquisite softness of the blue, from light azure to indigo in successive shades as the cavern penetrated deeper and deeper into the berg, with fringes of icicles hanging from the roof. Fancy slipping past an ice-cliff, and suddenly opening a scene such as this!"

This firing of the *Challenger's* 9-pounder actually took place on February 21st, 1874. Campbell tells of the incident (p. 114):

"Feb. 21—A beautiful sunny day, and dead calm. Ship lying motionless on a glass-like sea, large tabular bergs close around. In the afternoon we steamed alongside a high berg, from which, on one side, a ledge projected, terminating in a cliff some fifty feet high. When a short distance off we fired a 9-pounder Armstrong into this cliff. Bang! followed by a rattling crash as if the whole berg was coming down about our ears. For a depth of several feet, and a length of about ten yards, the whole face came cracking, splitting, and splashing down with a roar, making the water below white with foam and powdered ice. We then fired into the high upper cliff, which, being softer, the shot plunged into, leaving scarcely a mark. We got a fair photograph of this berg."

All, however, was not the calm and beautiful scene which Campbell describes here, for some three days later the *Challenger* had one run-in with and one narrow escape from large ice bergs (Campbell, pp. 116-117):

"Feb. 24—Hitherto we have had tolerably fine weather, nothing much to disturb our peace of mind except darkness, snow-squalls, and thick weather among icebergs. But now we are going to have a disagreeable change. During the night we hove to, and at four o'clock put the dredge over; but the wind suddenly coming on to blow fresh from the southward, the dredge was hove up in a hurry, by which time it was blowing a gale, with heavy snow-squalls and very thick weather. Having steam up we went under the lee of a sloping-sided berg, and treble-reefed the topsails. During this operation the eddy current carried the ship too near. Bump, bump! smash, crash! as the ship rose and fell with the swell, spearing the ice with the 'dolphin striker,' which, as well as one 'whisker' and the 'jib-boom,' carried away, leaving all the head-gear in a state of wreck, while the men aloft, thinking they would have the top-gallant-mast about their ears, scurried down with extraordinary activity.

"We then sheered off, hove to under storm-trysails, got steam up ready in four boilers, laid the yards ready for making a 'stern-board,' and so drifted along; the gale increasing fast, weather thick as pea-soup, and small, very hard snow pinging into one's face, like a shower of peas blown through a steam-blast. Temperature 22° (the coldest we experienced, but 22° with a 'whole gale' blowing over the pack feels very much colder than it sounds).

"We drifted on all forenoon, seeing no bergs through the fog and blinding showers of snow, though we knew that they were close around somewhere. In the meantime we were hard at work getting in the wreck of the head-gear—no easy work, in the intense cold and violent wind—when suddenly, at three o'clock, in the middle of a tremendous thick squall, comes the hail from the forecastle, 'Iceberg close to under the lee bow, Sir.' There is no room to steam ahead, so 'full speed astern!' Rattle, rattle, goes the screw, sixty revolutions a minute; 'Clear lower deck, make sail!' shriek the boatswain's mates; on deck flies everybody; 'Maintopmen aloft, loose the maintopsail!' 'Fore part, take in the fore-trysail!' The captain and commander howling out orders from the bridge, hardly heard in the roaring of the wind; officers repeating the howls. The weather-clew of the maintopsail is set aback, the headsails taken in, slowly she gathers stern way, keeping her head turning slightly towards the berg, a towering, dim white mass looming grimly through the driving snow, and then she clears it—a narrow shave!"

It is impossible to determine just which dredging operation Shephard is depicting here. Actually, the *Challenger* did no dredging during her half-day excursion below the Antarctic Circle (Feb. 16, 1874). Spry gave the account of the ship's short penetration below the Antarctic Circle (pp. 136-137):

"Feb. 16th—The weather was remarkably fine, such as is but seldom experienced in these high latitudes— bright sun and blue sky, with but little wind; so had recourse to steam, passing some magnificent icebergs, extending in all directions and in every conceivable shape and form; for the most part having flat tops covered with snow, glistening in the sun, with smooth, inaccessible sides, beautifully tinted with every shade of blue and green. It was about 1.30 P.M. when we crossed the barrier of the Antarctic Circle (latitude 66° 30′ south), in longitude 78° east, situated about 1400 miles from the South Pole. The sight was indeed a grand one as we threaded our way through the pack ice and up through avenues of vast bergs, over a course never before taken by explorers; all this left an impression of those icy desolate regions that can never be forgotten. It seems most difficult to attempt a description, for all I could say would convey but little of the reality to the imagination of one who has not been similarly situated. Proceeding on to latitude 66° 40′ south, the course was altered, and the horizon scanned in all directions for land; the weather was unusually clear, so that we should certainly have seen it had any existed within a considerable distance: none however was visible. The Circle was re-crossed, and we proceeded east along the margin of the great pack. The icebergs had now become so numerous that it was not unusual to be able to count over one hundred and fifty from the deck, and many of them appeared to be miles in length."

The *Challenger's* nearest dredge site to the Antarctic Circle was Station 153 two days earlier where they recovered blue mud at 65° 42′ S., 79° 49′ E., in 1675 fms. After turning north at 66° 40′ S., their southernmost point, they dredged several more times en route to Australia (Campbell, pp. 118-119):

"Feb. 26—Trawled in 1,975 fms.: a quantity of granite stones an umbellularia; a very large serolis—the nearest approach to the ancient trilobites known—about two inches long; sea-urchins, one of which has been got already in the north, but was then supposed to be a deformity; starfish; and four fish —one with glittering scales, of which only a few remained, the rest having been rubbed off by the net; and great numbers of large and small holothurians. . . . March 3—Trawled in 1,950 fms on white diatomaceous ooze. A great haul of holothurians, mud, starfish, shrimps, echinoderms, several umbellularia, a few fish, and a large stone with sea-anemones on it. No ice seen during the day.

"Mar. 4—To-day one berg was seen, and it proved to be the last. (Lat. 53° 17′ S., Long. 109° 23′ E.) The past three days we have had a series of gorgeous sunsets and sunrises, which being trite subjects, I will tell you only of one. Towards the evening, the sky being cloudy, a long low arch formed over the western horizon, spanning it to an altitude of 20°. Below this the sky was clear and blue, above cloudy, the boundary line of the arch misty, but distinct; and then, as the sun set, the blue seen through the arch became a pale apple-green, with small crimson clouds floating in it, while above the arch, the clouds became dark purple, flushed with crimson.

"We trawled three times more on our way to Melbourne; in 1,800, 2,150 and 2,600 fms., getting capital hauls each time. The bottom in the last sounding was red clay with nodules of manganese. We arrived at Melbourne on March the 17th, and so ended happily our Antarctic cruise."

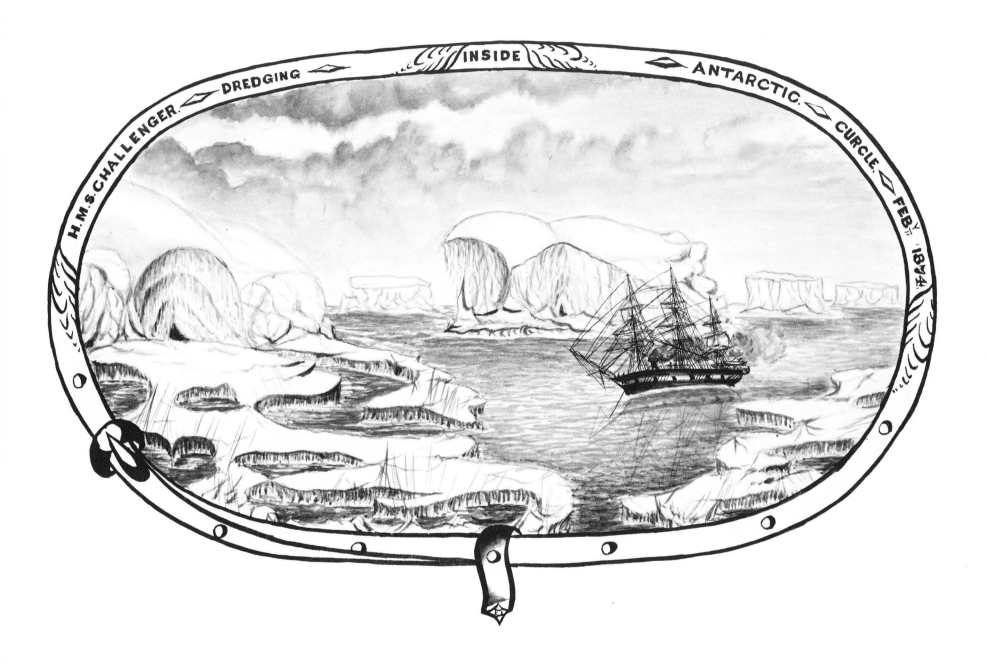

Epilogue

The last sketch in the sketchbook leaves the *Challenger* in the ice of the southernmost Indian Ocean. There were, however, two more oceans and twenty-six months of the *Challenger* expedition. The ship went on to Sydney, to New Zealand, the Tongas, Fijis, and on up through the Philippines to China. She came back south to New Guinea, north to Japan, east to the Hawaiian Islands, south to Tahiti, east to Chile, around the southern tip of South America through the Straits of Magellan, and up to Montevideo. The *Challenger* continued her multiple observations east to the Mid-Atlantic Ridge, and then turned north for the run to England, arriving off Spithead May 24, 1876.

It is hard to believe Shephard terminated his sketching activities just because one sketchbook was full by the time the ship reached Australia. Where, then, are the other sketchbooks of Benjamin Shephard, cooper and occasional coopers crew aboard the H.M.S. *Challenger?* Hopefully, someday they will be found and recognized for what they are. In the meantime, the world scientific community is indebted to an almost unknown crewman aboard the *Challenger* for adding a delightful new dimension to our knowledge and understanding of what still stands as the greatest marine scientific expedition of all times.

About the Authors

J. Welles Henderson is a Philadelphia lawyer who founded the Philadelphia Maritime Museum in 1960. A graduate of Princeton University and Harvard Law School, Mr. Henderson has devoted a portion of his practice to admiralty law. He is an Associate Editor of *American Maritime Cases*. From his childhood he was an avid collector of maritime memorabilia. This became the nucleus of the collection of the Philadelphia Maritime Museum which he served as president for 12 years until becoming Chairman of the Board in 1972. He is past president of the Port of Philadelphia Maritime Society, and received the Society's Annual Award for his efforts in behalf of the Port of Philadelphia. Mr. Henderson lectures widely and is the author of several papers on maritime history and art.

Harris B. Stewart, Jr., is Director of the Atlantic Oceanographic and Meteorological Laboratories, a Federal research complex of the U. S. Department of Commerce, on Virginia Key at Miami, Florida. An oceanographer himself, Dr. Stewart has participated in numerous scientific expeditions which have called at several of the ports visited by the *Challenger* during her famous four-year voyage of exploration. A graduate of Princeton University and the Scripps Institution of Oceanography of the University of California, he has published two books on the oceans, *The Global Sea* and *Deep Challenge*. He is a member of the Underwater Advisory Board of the Philadelphia Maritime Museum. Dr. Stewart was invited to make the first public presentation of *The Challenger Sketchbook* at the Challenger Expedition Centenary celebration held in Edinburgh, Scotland, September, 1972, in conjunction with the Second International Congress on the History of Oceanography.

About the Philadelphia Maritime Museum

The Philadelphia Maritime Museum is a non-profit charitable organization which operates a museum devoted to the history of the maritime industry, shipping and the sea. It is an accredited teaching museum, conducting a free lecture program for school children.

Its special collections include a 5000-volume research library; the pioneer "underwater" gallery comprehensively tracing the history of man under water; and the historic barkentine *Gazela Primeiro* built in Portugal in 1883 which was the last active square rigger of the Portuguese fishing fleet until she was retired in 1969.

In 1972, the Museum began renovation of a large building near Independence Hall in Philadelphia to provide completely modern facilities for the preservation, exhibition and educational use of its collections.